GRADE
2

Comprehension

Practice at 3 Levels ●●●

Table of Contents

Introduction

What Is Expected of Today's Students?

Educational standards for reading set the following key expectations:

- Students must comprehend increasingly complex texts in order to be ready for the demands of college and career-level reading.
- Students must read a diverse array of classic and contemporary literature from around the world as well as challenging informational texts in a range of subjects.

Students must demonstrate a gradually improved competency in comprehending, analyzing, and responding critically to three main text types: opinion/argument, informational, and narrative.

How Does This Book Help You Address These Expectations?

This book provides powerful mini-lessons and so much more! It features flexible, targeted mini-lessons plus guided and independent practice and assessment that helps students of all abilities reach rigorous on-grade-level expectations. The unique combination of rich mini-lessons, practice, and assessment provides step-by-step resources to build essential skills that meet today's academic standards.

What Is the Goal of *Meaningful Mini-Lessons & Practice: Comprehension*?

This book features a menu of short, purposeful mini-lessons together with guided and independent practice and assessment that builds students' competency in the following areas:

- Demonstrating independence
- Building strong content knowledge
- Responding to the varying demands of audience, task, purpose, and discipline
- Comprehending and critiquing
- Valuing evidence
- Using technology and digital media strategically and capably
- Understanding varying perspectives and cultures

What Is a Mini-Lesson, Anyway?

A mini-lesson provides concise and targeted instruction that breaks down a specific learning objective into chunked, manageable goals. Teachers are often short on time, and the mini-lesson approach allows for impactful instruction delivered in a concise format. It also allows students to practice skills in real-world contexts and take part in guided reflection on their learning experience. Mini-lessons often facilitate student collaboration through thinking, talking and reflecting together. They can be used for a variety of instructional topics and contexts, including intervention, English Learner, and special needs settings.

How Does This Book Help My Students?

Meaningful Mini-Lessons & Practice: Comprehension offers:

Three leveled, reproducible versions of each passage are provided so that below-grade-level students start their comprehension practice at their reading level. Repeated readings and teacher support scaffold students up to the on-grade-level passage. Struggling students do not miss out on essential comprehension practice because the comprehension questions can be answered no matter which passage is read. In order for students to progress to grade-level competency, it is recommended that once students build background on the topic, they move up to the on-grade-level passage, which includes richer vocabulary and language structures.

Levels L–M

Levels N–P

Levels Q–R

Gives the teacher the reading level of each of the three passages. See the chart on page 5.

An Overview page introduces each of the three sections and provides background on the text type and genres in that section. A graphic organizer is provided to help you introduce the text type.

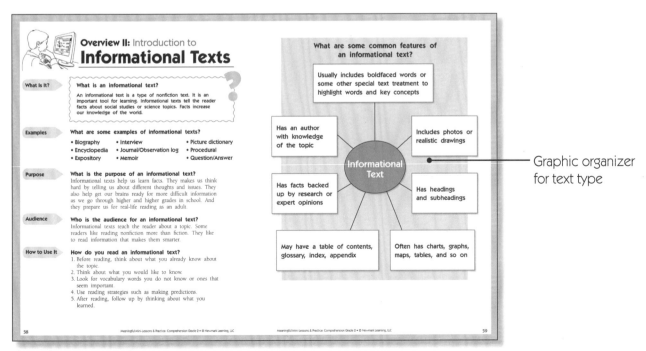

Graphic organizer for text type

Introductory spread

Each set of passages in a genre begins with a mini-lesson that consistently frames the specific details of the genre students are about to read. A reproducible graphic organizer is provided for you to share as is, or you can cover the answers and complete together or individually as a response to your mini-lesson.

Explanation of the genre

Graphic organizer to copy or project

Brief explanation of how this text is different from other types of text

Gives a purpose for this genre

Notes the audience for this type of text

Tips for comprehending this type of text

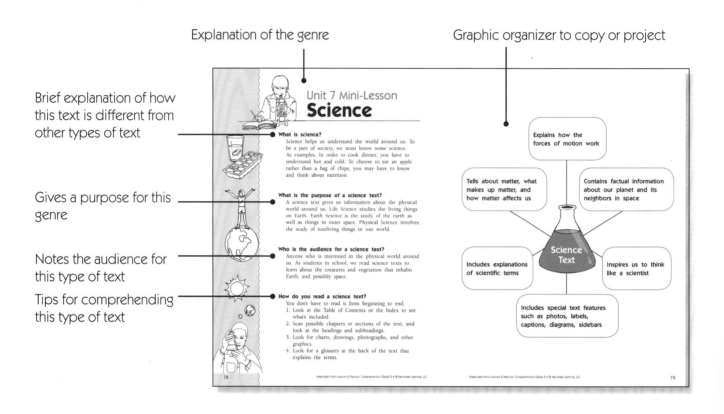

Text-dependent and critical-thinking questions appear after each set of passages. The questions are research-based and support reading skills and standards at grade level.

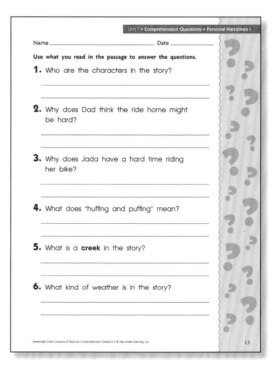

Students get rich text type and genre practice using an array of narrative texts, content-area informational texts in social studies and science, and opinion/argument texts.

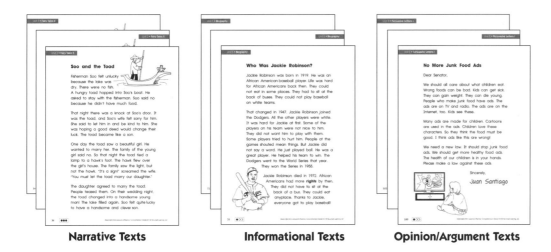

| Narrative Texts | Informational Texts | Opinion/Argument Texts |

Vocabulary is studied in context, per grade-level expectations.

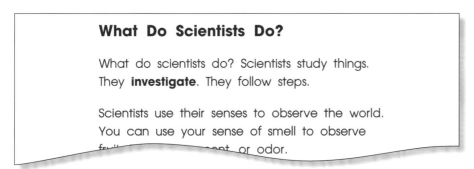

What Do Scientists Do?

What do scientists do? Scientists study things.
They **investigate**. They follow steps.

Scientists use their senses to observe the world.
You can use your sense of smell to observe

How Are the Passages Leveled?

The first passage is two grades below level, the second passage is one grade below level, and the third passage is on-grade level. Please refer to the chart below to see a correlation to letter levels and number levels.

Mini-Lessons Reading Levels

Level Icon	Grade 1		Grade 2		Grade 3		Grade 4		Grade 5		Grade 6	
●○○	A–C	1–4	D–E	5-8	F–I	9–16	L–M	24–28	N–P	30–38	Q–R	40
●●○	D–E	5–8	F–I	9–16	J–M	18–28	N–P	30–38	Q–R	40	S–U	44–50
●●●	F–I	9–16	J–M	18–28	N–P	30–38	Q–R	40	S–U	44–50	V–X	60

Overview I: Introduction to
Narrative Texts

What Is It?

What is a narrative text?

A narrative text is a real or fictional story that follows a pattern. That story starts by getting the reader's attention with an exciting or interesting beginning. At least one of the characters has a problem.

Examples

What are some examples of a narrative text?

- Adventure
- Animal fantasy
- Diary
- Fable
- Fairy tale
- Folktale
- Historical fiction
- Horror
- Humorous fiction
- Mystery
- Myth
- Play
- Realistic fiction
- Science fiction

Purpose

What is the purpose of a narrative text?

Basically, the purpose is to tell a story. Different types of narratives will have different purposes. For example, the purpose of a fable is to teach people lessons or explain mysteries of the earth.

Audience

Who is the audience for a narrative text?

The audience is any reader of that text. You may prefer certain types of narrative text to others. Sometimes you will enjoy a book because a character is like you. Sometimes you like a story because a character is NOTHING like you.

How to Use It

How do you read a narrative text?

1. Read from beginning to end.
2. Use a graphic organizer or highlighter to keep the characters straight.

Meaningful Mini-Lessons & Practice: Comprehension Grade 2 • © Newmark Learning, LLC

What are some common features of a narrative text?

A problem that makes you wonder what will happen

An exciting or interesting beginning

Details about characters, setting, and plot

Narrative Text

A main event that has action and emotion

Actions that lead to solving the problem

A good ending to the story

Unit 1 Mini-Lesson
Personal Narratives

What is a personal narrative?

A personal narrative is a true story about a real person's life. A personal narrative is usually told in the first person. That means it uses words such as *I*, *we*, *us*, *our*, etc. Most personal narratives are about something big in the author's life. For example, the story could be about winning an award.

What is the purpose of a personal narrative?

A personal narrative helps readers feel like they were there, with the writer. Writers accomplish this by using sensory details—what they saw, heard, touched, smelled, and tasted.

Who is the audience for a personal narrative?

People write personal narratives for all kinds of readers. Writers write them because they want to share something important that happened to them.

How do you read a personal narrative?

Ask yourself:
1. *Did this event happen to the person, or did the person make it happen?*
2. *How did this event affect the person's life?*
3. *Is the author simply writing to entertain, or is there something that I can learn from his or her experience?*

Meaningful Mini-Lessons & Practice: Comprehension Grade 2 • © Newmark Learning, LLC

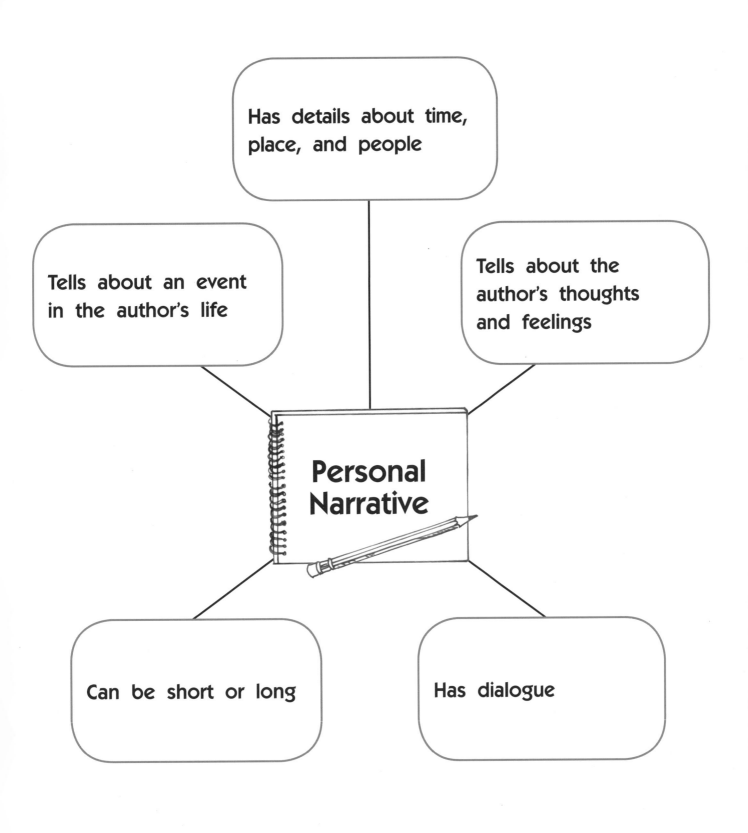

Has details about time, place, and people

Tells about an event in the author's life

Tells about the author's thoughts and feelings

Personal Narrative

Can be short or long

Has dialogue

The Bike Ride

The sun was out. The air was warm.
It was a nice day.

"Let's bike to the **creek**," I said. "It will be our
first one this year. The trees are in bloom. It
will be a pretty ride!"

"The ride home is up a hill," said Dad.
It might be too hard for you, Jada."

"No, I am in great shape," I said.

I put on my helmet. Then I rode up and
down the driveway. I was huffing and puffing.
"That was hard!" I said.

Dad laughed. "The problem is not you,"
he said. "It is your bike. Your tires are
almost flat."

Dad and I went to the garage.
He found his air pump. It
was on the wall. "This will
do the trick," he said.

●○○   *Meaningful Mini-Lessons & Practice: Comprehension Grade 2* • © Newmark Learning, LLC

The Bike Ride

The day was sunny and warm. It was perfect for riding bikes. "How about a bike ride, Dad?" I asked. "It will be our first one this year. We could ride to the **creek** and back. All the trees are in bloom. It will be a pretty ride!"

Dad looked at me. "That's a long uphill ride on the way home. It might be too hard for you."

"No, I'm in great shape," I said. I put on my helmet. Then I began to pedal up and down the driveway. Soon I was huffing and puffing. "Maybe I'm not in such good shape after all!" I said.

Dad laughed. "The problem is not you," he said. "Your tires are almost flat."

So, Dad and I went out to the garage. He took his air pump off the wall. "This will do the trick," he said.

The Bike Ride

The sun was shining and the air was warm.
It was a perfect day for the first bike ride of
the year. "How about it, Dad?" I asked. "We
could ride to the **creek** and back. It will be
such a pretty ride with the trees in bloom!"

Dad frowned. "That's a long uphill ride on the
way home. It might be a little too much for
you on the first time out."

"No," I replied. "I'm in great shape." With that,
I wheeled out my bike and strapped on my
helmet. Then I began to pedal up and down
the long dirt driveway.

I came back inside after five minutes, huffing
and puffing. "Maybe I'm not in such
good shape after all!" I gasped.

Dad just laughed. "The problem
isn't you, it's your flat tires."

Dad and I found his air
pump hanging on a wall
in the garage. "This will do
the trick," he said.

●●●

Name _____ Date _____

Use what you read in the passage to answer the questions.

1. Who are the characters in the story?

_____

_____

2. Why does Dad think the ride home might be hard?

_____

_____

3. Why does Jada have a hard time riding her bike?

_____

_____

4. What does "huffing and puffing" mean?

_____

_____

5. What is a **creek** in the story?

_____

_____

6. What kind of weather is in the story?

_____

_____

A Visit to the Dentist

Ben, Tyler, and I went to the dentist. It was time to get our teeth cleaned. Ben and I had been many times. But Tyler had not. He was afraid.

Dr. Huber met us in the waiting room. "Who's first?" he asked.

"NOT ME!" Tyler said.

Mom said something to Dr. Huber. He nodded. "He'll be fine," he said. "We'll go from oldest to youngest. Let's go, Ellie."

Dr. Huber finished cleaning my teeth. Then he showed me the prize box. I saw a jump rope I wanted. But then I got a great idea. I took a toy car. I went out to Tyler.

"That was fun," I said to Tyler. "Dr. Huber used bubble gum toothpaste. Then I got this toy car for a prize!"

Tyler jumped up. "Let me go next! Please!"

A Visit to the Dentist

Today Ben, Tyler, and I went to the dentist. It was time to get our teeth cleaned. Ben and I had been to the dentist many times. We weren't worried, but this was Tyler's first visit.

Dr. Huber met us in the waiting room. "Who's first?" he asked.

"NOT ME!" Tyler said loudly.

Mom whispered something to Dr. Huber. He nodded. "He'll be fine," he said. Then he said, "Ellie, we'll go from oldest to youngest."

Dr. Huber finished cleaning my teeth. Then he showed me the prize box. I came up with a plan and took a toy car to the waiting room.

"That was fun," I said to Tyler. "Dr. Huber used bubble-gum-flavored toothpaste. Then I got this toy car for a prize!"

Tyler jumped out of his seat. "Let me go next! Please, please!" he said.

A Visit to the Dentist

Today Ben, Tyler, and I went to the dentist. Ben and I had been to the dentist many times. We had an appointment for our teeth to be cleaned. Tyler was pretty nervous.

Dr. Huber met us in the waiting room. "Who's first?" he asked.

"NOT ME!" Tyler said loudly.

Mom whispered something to Dr. Huber. He nodded and said, "He'll be fine. We'll go from oldest to youngest. Ellie?"

When Dr. Huber finished cleaning my teeth, he showed me the prize box. I started to take a jump rope, but then I reached for a toy car instead. I walked out to the waiting room.

"Boy, that was fun," I said to Tyler. "Dr. Huber used bubble-gum-flavored toothpaste, and then I got a prize. A toy car!"

That's when Tyler jumped out of his seat. "Let me go next, please, please!" he said.

●●●

Name _____ Date _____

Use what you read in the passage to answer the questions.

1. Where did the children go?

_____

_____

2. Who was the oldest of the three children?

_____

_____

3. How was Tyler feeling about visiting the dentist? Why?

_____

_____

4. What flavor toothpaste did Ellie get?

_____

_____

5. Do you think the dentist and Mom had a plan? Why do you think that?

_____

_____

6. What did you think the author was trying to tell the reader?

_____

_____

Realistic Fiction

What is realistic fiction?

Realistic fiction consists of stories that COULD happen in everyday life. But they are not true. They are made up. The settings are real. The setting might be a familiar place such as a home, school, office, or farm. The stories involve some type of conflict, or problem.

What is the purpose of realistic fiction?

Realistic fiction shows how people deal with successes and failures. It shows:
1. how people make decisions
2. how people develop relationships
3. how people solve problems

Who is the audience for realistic fiction?

A writer writes realistic fiction for anyone who likes to read. Kids, teens, adults, and seniors like to read about fun, mysterious, or exciting things that happen to made-up characters.

How do you read realistic fiction?

1. The title will give you a clue about an important character or problem in the story.
2. As you read, think about the thoughts, feelings, and actions of the main characters.
3. Pay attention to how the characters change in the story.

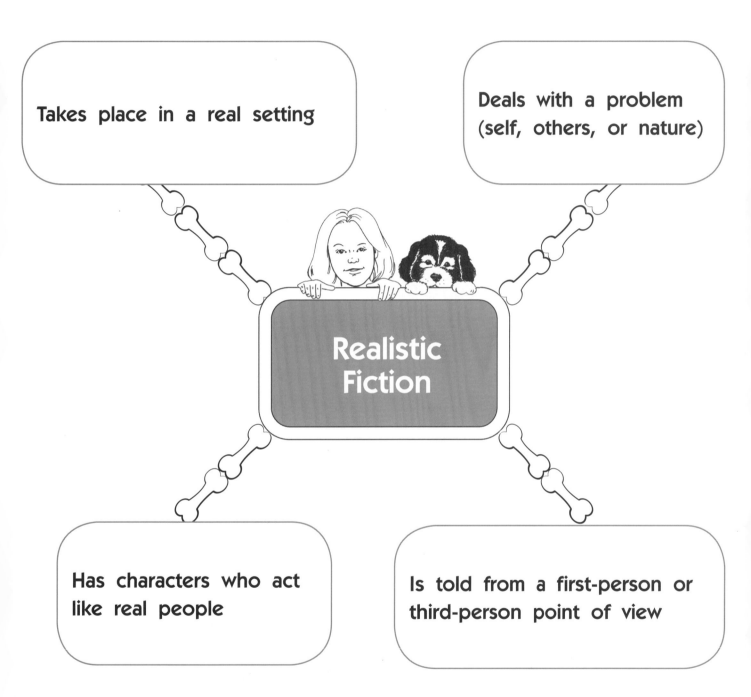

Takes place in a real setting

Deals with a problem (self, others, or nature)

Realistic Fiction

Has characters who act like real people

Is told from a first-person or third-person point of view

Mr. Willis's Bricks

Jamal looked outside. He saw Mr. Willis. Mr. Willis was making a brick wall. Jamal watched for a while. He walked over to Mr. Willis's yard.

"Hi, Mr. Willis," said Jamal. "Are you making a wall?"

"I am," said Mr. Willis. "The wall is for my garden. You can keep me company. I'm going to keep working, though. I want to get this done by the weekend."

"How did you make those bricks?" asked Jamal.

"I use red **clay** from the ground," Mr. Willis said. "Then I add some water. It gets like thick mud. I add straw next. Then I put the mixture in a mold. It dries in the sun. I take the mold off. Then I let the bricks dry some more."

"That's cool!" Jamal said. "Next time, can I help?"

Mr. Willis's Bricks

Jamal looked out the window. He saw his neighbor, Mr. Willis. Mr. Willis was making a brick wall for his garden. Jamal watched for a while. Then his curiosity got the best of him. He walked over to Mr. Willis's backyard.

"Hi, Mr. Willis," said Jamal. "Are you making another wall?"

"I am," said Mr. Willis. "You're welcome to keep me company. I'm going to keep working so I get this done by the weekend."

"How did you create those bricks?" asked Jamal.

"I use red **clay** from the ground," Mr. Willis began. "Then I add some water. It gets like thick mud. I add straw next. Then I put the mixture in a mold. It dries in the sun. I take the mold off and let the bricks dry some more. And that's it!"

"That's really cool!" Jamal said. "Next time, can I help?"

Mr. Willis's Bricks

Jamal looked outside and saw Mr. Willis making a brick wall. Jamal watched for a while. Then his curiosity got the best of him. He made his way to Mr. Willis's yard.

"Hi, Mr. Willis," said Jamal. "Are you building a wall with homemade bricks?"

"I am," said Mr. Willis. "The wall is for my garden. You can keep me company. I'm going to keep working, though. I want to get this done by the weekend."

"How did you create those bricks?" asked Jamal.

"I use red **clay** from the ground that I specially prepare," Mr. Willis said. "I add some water to make a thick mud. Then I add straw next. I put the mixture in a mold. I let it dry and bake in the sun. I take the mold off. Then I let the bricks dry some more. And that's it!"

"That's cool!" Jamal said. "Next time, can I please be your helper?"

●●●

Name _____ Date _____

Use what you read in the passage to answer the questions.

1. What is Mr. Willis doing?

_____

_____

2. What does Mr. Willis use the bricks for?

_____

_____

3. What is **clay**?

_____

_____

4. Why is it good that Mr. Willis lives in a hot, sunny place?

_____

_____

5. What does Jamal want to do "next time"?

_____

_____

6. What would happen to the bricks if Mr. Willis forgot a step?

_____

_____

The Tree House

Jake woke up with a great idea. He would build a **tree house**. "I want to build a tree house! Is that okay?" he asked his dad.

"That's a great idea," said Dad. "I'll help you!"

Jake and Dad went out to the oak tree. They figured out what they would need. Then they got some boards. They got some nails. They sawed and sawed. The pieces were finally ready. Jake climbed up the tree. Dad handed him the boards. They nailed them to some thick branches.

Jake and his dad worked hard. They even put a roof on the tree house. They got done just before dark.

Jake found his brother. "Can I borrow a sleeping bag?" he asked.

"Sure," said Pete. "But can I come with you?"

Jake smiled. They both went to get ready.

● ○ ○

The Tree House

One morning Jake woke up with a great idea. He would build a **tree house**! "I want to build a tree house. Is that okay?" he asked his dad.

"It's not only okay," said Dad, "I'll even help you build it."

The two of them went out to the oak tree. They figured out what they would need. Then they got some boards and started sawing. The pieces were finally ready. Jake climbed up in the tree. Dad handed him the boards. They nailed the boards to some thick branches.

Jake and his dad worked all day. They even put a roof over the tree house. Now it would stay dry in the rain. They finished just before dark.

That night, Jake talked to his brother. "Can I borrow a sleeping bag?" he asked.

"Sure," said Pete. "But can I come with you?" Jake smiled. They both got ready.

The Tree House

One morning when Jake woke up, he had a wonderful idea. He would build a **tree house**! "Is it okay if I build a tree house in the old oak?" he asked his dad.

"It's not only okay," said Dad, "I'll even help you build it."

The two of them went out to the oak tree after breakfast. They figured out what they would need. Then they got some boards and started sawing. When the pieces were ready, Jake climbed up in the tree. Dad handed him the boards. They nailed them to some sturdy branches.

Jake and his dad worked all day. They even put a roof over the tree house. That way it would stay dry in the rain. They finally finished just before dark.

That night, Jake talked to his brother. "Can I borrow a sleeping bag?" he asked.

"Sure," said Pete. "But can I come with you?" Jake smiled and they got ready.

●●●

Name _____ Date _____

Use what you read in the passage to answer the questions.

1. What is a **tree house**?

_____

_____

2. Does the story take place in the day or the night?

_____

_____

3. Does Dad think the tree house is a good idea? What makes you think that?

_____

_____

4. What is the first thing Jake and Dad have to do to build the tree house?

_____

_____

5. What are two things Jake and his dad need in order to build the tree house?

_____

_____

6. Why did Jake borrow a sleeping bag?

_____

_____

Unit 3 Mini-Lesson
Fairy Tales

What is a fairy tale?

A fairy tale is a story about long ago. In fact, many fairy tales start with the words "Once upon a time." A fairy tale usually has:

- characters who are good
- characters who are evil
- characters who have magical powers

Even an animal or an object, such as a tree or a rock, can be magical. Many fairy tales include kings, queens, princes, and princesses. Some of the tales have imaginary creatures such as dragons, fairies, giants, and ogres.

What is the purpose of a fairy tale?

In a fairy tale, the storyteller often teaches a lesson. Most fairy tales make people feel good at the end since the good characters almost always live "happily ever after."

Who is the audience for a fairy tale?

The audience can be anyone. Children make up a large part of a fairy tale's audience.

How do you read a fairy tale?

1. Figure out who the "good guys" and "bad guys" are.
2. Try to predict how the good guys will be rewarded and how the bad guys will be punished.
3. Be prepared for some magical surprises along the way!

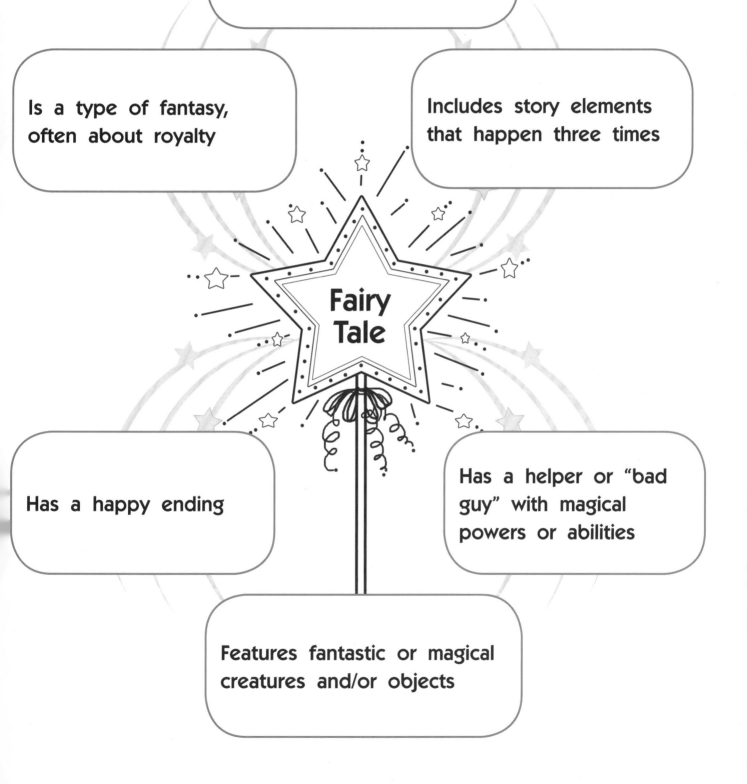

Has a character who gets help from another character

Is a type of fantasy, often about royalty

Includes story elements that happen three times

Fairy Tale

Has a happy ending

Has a helper or "bad guy" with magical powers or abilities

Features fantastic or magical creatures and/or objects

The Story of Yen

Yen did all of the **chores**. Her stepmother gave her one bowl of rice a day. One day, Yen took her rice down to the pond. She started to cry. Her tears fell on the pond. A small goldfish swam to her. It opened its mouth.

"You must be starving, too," said Yen. She gave the fish some of her rice.

Yen talked to the fish every day. Her stepmother saw her one day. That night she said to Yen, "You work hard. Here's your supper." The fish was on the plate.

Yen buried the fish. She had a dream. The fish told her that it had "wishing bones."

The king had a party. Yen could not go. She dug up the bones. Then she made a wish. The bones became a dress and golden slippers. Yen went to the party. She saw the king. It was love at first sight.

Yen and the king were married. Her stepmother was never allowed to visit.

●○○

The Story of Yen

Yen did all of the **chores**. Her stepmother gave her one bowl of rice a day. One day, Yen took her meal down to the fish pond. She started to cry. Her tears fell on the pond. A small goldfish swam to her. It opened its mouth.

"I see that you are starving, too," said Yen. She gave the goldfish some of her rice.

Yen visited the goldfish every day. One day, her stepmother saw Yen talking to the fish. That night her stepmother said, "You work hard. I've cooked you supper." The goldfish was on the dish.

Yen buried her friend. She dreamed about the fish. It told her that it had "wishing bones."

The king had a party. Yen was not allowed to go. She dug up the bones and made a wish. The bones became a lovely dress and golden slippers. Yen went to the party. She saw the king, and it was love at first sight! Yen and the king were married. Her stepmother wasn't allowed to visit.

The Story of Yen

Yen did all of the **chores** at home. Her stepmother gave her one bowl of rice a day. One day, Yen took her meal down to the fish pond. Yen's big, wet tears fell on the pond. A small goldfish swam to her with its mouth open.

"I see that you are starving, too," said Yen. She shared some of her rice.

Yen visited the goldfish every day. One day, her stepmother saw Yen talking to the fish. That night her stepmother said, "You've been working hard, so I cooked you supper." On the dish lay the goldfish.

Yen buried her friend. In a dream, the fish told her that it had "wishing bones."

The king had a party. Yen was not allowed to go. She dug up the bones and made a wish. The bones became a lovely dress and golden slippers. Yen went to the party, saw the king, and it was love at first sight! Yen and the king were married. Her stepmother wasn't allowed to visit.

●●●

Name _____ Date _____

Use what you read in the passage to answer the questions.

1. What are **chores** in the tale?

_____

_____

2. Why does Yen share her rice with the goldfish?

_____

_____

3. What happened to the goldfish?

_____

_____

4. What story do you know that is like this one?

_____

_____

5. What is similar about this story and the one you know? What is different?

_____

_____

6. What message is the author trying to give the reader?

_____

_____

Soo and the Toad

Fisherman Soo felt unlucky. The lake dried up. There were no fish. A hungry toad hopped into Soo's boat. He asked to stay with the fisherman. Soo said no. He did not think they had enough food.

That night there was a knock on Soo's door. It was the toad. Soo's wife felt bad for him. She said they should be kind. She hoped a good deed would bring luck. Soo and his wife cared for the toad like a son.

One day the toad saw a girl. He wanted to marry her. The family of the young girl said no. So that night the toad tied a lamp to a hawk's foot. The hawk flew over the girl's house. The family saw the light. They did not see the hawk. The wife thought it was a sign. Their daughter should marry the toad.

People laughed at the girl. That night, the toad changed into a handsome young man! Soon water and fish filled the lake. Soo felt lucky. He had a handsome and clever son.

●○○

Soo and the Toad

Fisherman Soo felt unlucky. The lake was dry and had no fish. A hungry toad hopped into Soo's boat. He asked to stay with the fisherman. Soo said no because he didn't have much food.

That night there was a knock on Soo's door. It was the toad. Soo's wife felt sorry for him. She said to let him in and be kind to him. She was hoping their luck would change. Soo and his wife cared for the toad like a son.

One day the toad saw a pretty girl. He wanted to marry her. The family of the young girl said no. So, that night the toad tied a lamp to a hawk's foot. The hawk flew over the girl's house. The family saw the light, but not the hawk. The wife said it was a sign. She realized their daughter must marry the toad.

The daughter and the toad married. People laughed at them. That night, the toad changed into a handsome young man! The lake filled with water and fish. Soo felt lucky to have such a handsome and clever son.

Soo and the Toad

Fisherman Soo felt unlucky because the lake was dry. There were no fish. A hungry toad hopped into Soo's boat. He asked to stay with the fisherman. Soo said no because he didn't have much food.

That night there was a knock at Soo's door. It was the toad, and Soo's wife felt sorry for him. She said to let him in and be kind to him. She was hoping a good deed would change their luck. The toad became like a son.

One day the toad saw a beautiful girl. He wanted to marry her. The family of the young girl said no. So that night the toad tied a lamp to a hawk's foot. The hawk flew over the girl's house. The family saw the light, but not the hawk. "It's a sign!" screamed the wife. "You must let the toad marry our daughter."

The daughter agreed to marry the toad. People teased them. On their wedding night, the toad changed into a handsome young man! The lake filled again. Soo felt quite lucky to have a handsome and clever son.

●●●

Name _____ Date _____

Use what you read in the passage to answer the questions.

1. Why are there no fish?

_____

_____

2. Why does Fisherman Soo feel unlucky?

_____

_____

3. Why does Soo's wife want to help the toad?

_____

_____

4. Why do you think the girl is willing to marry the toad?

_____

_____

5. Why does Fisherman Soo feel lucky?

_____

_____

6. Could this story be true? Why or why not?

_____

_____

What is a fable?

A fable is a very short story. All fables teach a lesson, or moral. In most fables, the characters are animals.

What is the purpose of a fable?

Fables teach people lessons. Fables point out *foibles* that people have. A foible is a character flaw. Being boastful is a flaw. Being dishonest is also a flaw. Fables show why the flaw is bad. Fables are also fun to read. Their characters often do silly and foolish things.

Who is the audience for a fable?

People have told fables for thousands of years. Ancient peoples around the world all told fables. Later, in the Middle Ages, people continued this way of storytelling. Many people enjoy reading a fable and trying to figure out its moral. Fables are often read by schoolchildren when values are being discussed as part of a classroom lesson.

How do you read a fable?

1. The title will tell you who the main characters are.
2. Each character stands for ways that people behave or act. Ask yourself: *What trait does each character show?*
3. Note what happens to the main characters. Think about how what happens teaches the moral. Then try to figure out the moral is if it's not stated directly.

Has at least one character with a flaw or problem

Includes main characters that are usually animals

Has a character that learns a lesson

Fable

Is short

Has a moral, or lesson, at the end

The Lion and the Mouse

It was a long time ago. A lion was asleep in the woods. He was having a very good dream. But then a mouse ran across his paw. It woke the lion up. The lion reached out. He caught the little mouse and was about to eat him. But the mouse said, "Oh, please, great lion, don't eat me. Someday I might help you."

The lion thought this was funny. How could a mouse help him? But he was feeling good. So he let the mouse go.

Then some hunters saw the lion. They caught the lion in a net. They tied him down with ropes. Then they left to get a wagon. They were going to take the lion away.

The mouse came by and saw the lion. He started to **gnaw** on the ropes. Soon the ropes were gnawed through. The lion was freed.

"Thank you, my friend," said the lion. "You did help me after all."

The Lion and the Mouse

Once a lion was sleeping in the shade of the trees. He was having a very fine dream. But then a mouse ran across his paw. It woke the lion up. The lion reached out and caught the mouse. He was about to eat the little creature. But the mouse said, "Oh, please, great lion, don't eat me. Someday I might help you."

The lion thought this was funny. But he was in a good mood. He let the mouse go.

A few days later, some hunters entered the woods. They caught the lion in a net. They tied him down with ropes. Then they left to get a wagon to carry the lion away.

The mouse came by and saw the lion. He started to **gnaw** on the ropes. Soon the ropes were gnawed through. The lion was freed.

"Thank you, my small friend," said the lion. "You did help me after all."

●●○ 41

The Lion and the Mouse

One day long ago, a lion lay sleeping in the shade of the trees. He was having a very fine dream. But then a mouse ran across his paw and woke him up. The lion reached out and caught the mouse. He was about to eat the little creature. But the mouse said, "Oh, please, great lion, don't eat me. Someday I might help you."

The lion thought this was funny. But he was in a good mood, so he let the mouse go.

A few days later, several hunters entered the woods. They caught the lion in a net and tied him down with ropes. Then they went off to get a wagon to carry the lion away.

While the hunters were gone, the mouse came by and saw the lion. Right away, he started to **gnaw** on the ropes. Very quickly, he chewed through the ropes and set the lion free.

"Thank you, my small friend," said the lion. "You did help me after all."

Name _____ Date _____

Use what you read in the passage to answer the questions.

1. What was the lion doing when he met the mouse?

_____

_____

2. Why did the lion think what the mouse said was funny?

_____

_____

3. What does **gnaw** mean?

_____

_____

4. How was the mouse a friend to the lion?

_____

_____

5. How are the lion and the mouse similar?

_____

_____

6. What is the moral of this story?

_____

_____

The Horse and the Mule

A farmer had a mule and a horse. The farmer put his corn in some baskets. He tied some of the baskets to the horse. He tied the rest to the mule. He led the two down the road. It was market day.

Soon they came to a **steep** hill. The mule went up the hill quickly. The horse had to slow down. Then it stopped.

"I need help," the horse told the mule. "Please take part of my load."

"No, I won't," said the mule. "My load is heavy, too."

The horse took a few more steps. It slipped and fell. So the farmer took the baskets from the horse. He tied them to the mule. He and the mule started walking. He let the horse rest.

I am a fool, the mule thought. *I would not help the horse. Now I have to take all of it myself.*

Meaningful Mini-Lessons & Practice: Comprehension Grade 2 • © Newmark Learning, LLC

The Horse and the Mule

A farmer had a mule and a horse. One day the farmer filled some baskets with corn. He tied some of the baskets to the horse. He tied the rest to the mule. Then he led the animals along the road to the market.

Soon they came to a **steep** hill. The mule went up the hill quickly. The horse slowed to a stop.

"I need help," the horse told the mule. "Please take part of my load."

"No, I won't," said the mule. "My load is heavy enough."

The horse took a few more steps. It slipped and fell. So the farmer took the baskets from the horse. He tied them to the mule. He and the mule started walking. He let the horse rest.

I am a fool, the mule thought. *I would not give the horse a little help. Now I must take the whole load myself.*

The Horse and the Mule

A farmer had a mule and a horse. One day the farmer filled some baskets with corn. He tied some of the baskets to the horse. He tied the rest to the mule. Then he led the animals along the road to the market.

Soon they came to a **steep** hill. The mule went up the hill quickly, but the horse slowed to a stop.

"I need help," the horse told the mule. "Please take part of my load."

"No, I won't," said the mule. "My load is heavy enough."

The horse took a few more steps, but then it slipped and fell. With that, the farmer took the baskets from the horse's back. He tied them to the mule and started off again for the market. He left the horse to rest beside the road.

What a fool I am, the mule thought. *I would not give the horse a little help, and now I must carry the whole load myself.*

●●●

Name _____ Date _____

Use what you read in the passage to answer the questions.

1. Where are the farmer, the horse, and the mule going?

_____

_____

2. What do you think the farmer is going to do with his corn?

_____

_____

3. What does **steep** mean in the fable?

_____

_____

4. How are the horse and mule similar? How are they different?

_____

_____

5. What does the farmer do that gives you a clue as to what kind of person he is?

_____

_____

6. What is the moral of the story?

_____

_____

Unit 5 Mini-Lesson
Trickster Tales

What is a trickster tale?

A trickster tale is a short story. In a trickster tale, animals or other creatures talk. They think and act like people. The trickster uses clever tricks or traps to fool another character. The trickster is often much smaller than the character he or she fools. Sometimes the trickster wants to help others. Other times the trickster only wants to help himself or herself.

What is the purpose of a trickster tale?

A trickster tale shows how people act and how they deal with their problems in an entertaining way. A trickster tale often teaches a lesson. The tale shows what happens when people make bad choices. Some of the bad choices come from the tricksters themselves!

Who is the audience for a trickster tale?

Trickster tales were originally passed down through storytelling. Most people love trickster tales and like to read them or hear them. Many trickster tales have been made into books and movies. Some of today's popular cartoon characters are tricksters!

How do you read a trickster tale?

Pay attention to the title. The title will often tell you which character is the trickster. Each character acts in ways that people do. As you read, ask yourself, *What human quality, or trait, does each character stand for or act like?* Notice what happens to the main characters. Think about how the events in the story help teach the lesson.

Meaningful Mini-Lessons & Practice: Comprehension Grade 2 • © Newmark Learning, LLC

Has a character with a flaw

Has main characters that are usually animals

Has a character with a problem

Trickster Tale

Is short and usually funny

Has a trickster who outwits another character

Fox and Raccoon

Fox and Raccoon were friends. They liked to play tricks on each other. Both had a special power. They could change forms.

"I am so smart," said Fox. "You cannot top me."

"I can too," said Raccoon. He thought and thought. "Look for me when the sun comes up," he said. "I will be on the road. I will show myself as a great lord."

Fox laughed. The next day, Fox stood by the road. A great lord walked by. His people were behind him. "Don't listen to him," Fox said. "He's not a lord. He's Raccoon. He turned himself into a lord. He's trying to trick us."

Raccoon had been hiding. He came out from his hiding place. The great lord laughed. Raccoon had not changed form. He had tricked Fox. "Thank you, great lord. You have been a big help," said Raccoon.

"Both of us are **tricksters**," Raccoon said. "But I just proved I'm the best."

Fox and Raccoon

Fox and Raccoon were friends. They liked to play tricks on each other. Both animals had a special power. They could change themselves into anything.

"I am so smart," said Fox. "You can't beat me."

"I will," said Raccoon. He thought for a second. Then he said, "Look for me tomorrow. I will be on the side of the road. I will take the form of a great lord."

Fox laughed. The next day, Fox stood by the road. A great lord led a line of his people. Fox said. "That's no lord. That's Raccoon. He's turned himself into a lord. He thinks he can trick us."

Raccoon came out from behind a tree. The great lord laughed. Raccoon had not turned himself into a great lord. He had tricked Fox. "Thank you, great lord," said Raccoon.

"That proves who the best **trickster** really is," Raccoon said to Fox.

Fox and Raccoon

Fox and Raccoon were friends, and they liked to play tricks on each other, too. Both animals had a special power. They could change themselves into anything they wished.

"I am so clever," said Fox. "You can't beat me."

"I will," said Raccoon. He thought for a second. Then he said, "Look for me tomorrow. I will be on the side of the road and will take the form of a great lord."

Fox chuckled. The next day, Fox waited by the road. A great lord led a line of his people. Fox called out to everyone. "That's no lord. That's Raccoon. He's turned himself into a lord. He thinks he can trick us."

Raccoon came out of hiding. The great lord laughed. Raccoon had not turned himself into a great lord, he only tricked Fox into thinking that he had. "You have been a big help," said Raccoon to the lord. To Fox he said, "I guess that proves who the best **trickster** really is."

●●●

Name _____ Date _____

Use what you read in the passage to answer the questions.

1. What is the special power shared by Fox and Raccoon?

_____

_____

2. What is a **trickster**?

_____

_____

3. Why does the great lord laugh when Raccoon comes out of hiding?

_____

_____

4. What do you think of friends who play tricks on each other?

_____

_____

5. Is Raccoon the best trickster? Why?

_____

_____

6. What features does this story contain that make it a trickster tale?

_____

_____

The Poor Man and the Soup

A poor man did not eat for two days. He smelled fresh soup. He saw people at tables. Soup was on the stove. The owner came to the window. "What are you doing?" he asked.

"I am smelling your soup. It smells good," the poor man said.

"What?" yelled the owner. "You cannot stand at my window. You must pay me! Or you must wash my dishes. You must pay to smell my soup!"

Then the mayor came in. "I will pay for him," he said. The mayor dropped some coins onto the table. Then he scooped the coins up. He put them in his pocket.

"Why did you do that?" asked the owner.

"I paid you," said the mayor. "The *sound* of coins is payment for the *smell* of soup."

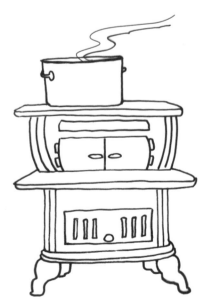

●○○   *Meaningful Mini-Lessons & Practice: Comprehension Grade 2* • © Newmark Learning, LLC

The Poor Man and the Soup

A poor man had not eaten for two days. He smelled fresh soup on a stove. People were eating soup at tables. The restaurant owner came to the window. "What are you doing?" he asked.

"I am enjoying the smell of your soup," the poor man said.

"See here," said the owner. "You cannot stand at my window. You cannot smell for free. You must pay me! You must wash my dishes. You must pay me to smell my soup!"

Then the mayor came in. "I will pay for this poor man." The mayor then dropped each coin onto the table. Then he scooped up the coins. He put them in his pocket.

"What do you mean by that?" asked the owner.

"That was your payment," said the mayor.

"The *sound* of coins is payment for the *smell* of soup," said the mayor.

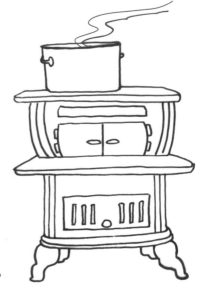

The Poor Man and the Soup

A poor man had not eaten for two days. The smell of fresh soup came from a nearby restaurant. The restaurant owner came to the window. "What are you doing?" he asked.

"I am enjoying the smell of your soup," the poor man said.

"You can't just smell my soup," said the owner. "You must pay me by washing dishes. You must pay me for smelling my soup."

Then the mayor appeared. "I will pay for this poor man," he said, standing tall.

The mayor dropped some coins onto a table, and then picked them up. He returned the coins to his pocket.

"What do you mean by that?" asked the restaurant owner.

"That was your payment," answered the mayor.

"The *sound* of coins is payment for the *smell* of soup," said the mayor.

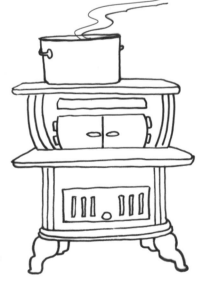

●●●   *Meaningful Mini-Lessons & Practice: Comprehension Grade 2* • © Newmark Learning, LLC

Name _____ Date _____

Use what you read in the passage to answer the questions.

1. Why is the poor man smelling the soup?

_____

_____

2. Why doesn't the restaurant owner want the man standing by his window?

_____

_____

3. How does the mayor trick the restaurant owner?

_____

_____

4. How would you describe the restaurant owner?

_____

_____

5. How do you think the author feels about greedy people? Why?

_____

_____

6. How is this story NOT like a typical trickster tale?

_____

_____

Overview II: Introduction to
Informational Texts

What Is It?

What is an informational text?

An informational text is a type of nonfiction text. It is an important tool for learning. Informational texts tell the reader facts about social studies or science topics. Facts increase our knowledge of the world.

Examples

What are some examples of informational texts?

- Biography
- Encyclopedia
- Expository
- Interview
- Journal/Observation log
- Memoir
- Picture dictionary
- Procedural
- Question/Answer

Purpose

What is the purpose of an informational text?

Informational texts help us learn facts. They makes us think hard by telling us about different thoughts and issues. They also help get our brains ready for more difficult information as we go through higher and higher grades in school. And they prepare us for real-life reading as an adult.

Audience

Who is the audience for an informational text?

Informational texts teach the reader about a topic. Some readers like reading nonfiction more than fiction. They like to read information that makes them smarter.

How to Use It

How do you read an informational text?

1. Before reading, think about what you already know about the topic.
2. Think about what you would like to know.
3. Look for vocabulary words you do not know or ones that seem important.
4. Use reading strategies such as making predictions.
5. After reading, follow up by thinking about what you learned.

What are some common features of an informational text?

Usually includes boldfaced words or some other special text treatment to highlight words and key concepts

Has an author with knowledge of the topic

Includes photos or realistic drawings

Informational Text

Has facts backed up by research or expert opinions

Has headings and subheadings

May have a table of contents, glossary, index, appendix

Often has charts, graphs, maps, tables, and so on

Unit 6 Mini-Lesson
Social Studies

What is social studies?

In social studies, we learn about the people in our world and how they relate to one another. We learn how they:

- live
- manage their communities
- relate to other groups

Learning these things helps give us the skills we need to be good citizens.

What is the purpose of a social studies text?

A social studies text gives us information about history. We read about history so we know how the countries of the world and the people in them grew to what and where we are now.

Who is the audience for a social studies text?

Anyone who is interested in people and culture makes a good audience for social studies texts. As students in school, we read social studies texts to learn about the world and where and how we fit in.

How do you read a social studies text?

1. You don't have to read it from beginning to end the way you read fiction.
2. Look at the Table of Contents or the Index to see what's included.
3. Scan possible chapters or sections of the text, and look at the headings and subheadings.
4. Are there charts, drawings, photographs, and other graphics? They provide information, too.
5. Look for important words, which often appear in boldface type or italics.
6. Look for a glossary at the back of the text that explains the terms.

Shows how people manage themselves and work together as a society

Compares people's similarities and differences

Shows how different people live their lives

Tells about people and groups of people

Social Studies Text

Shows how governments are run

Helps teach us how to participate as citizens in a society

Encourages us to make judgments about issues

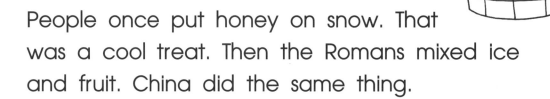

A Cold Treat

How old is ice cream? Who made it first? No one knows.

People once put honey on snow. That was a cool treat. Then the Romans mixed ice and fruit. China did the same thing.

Soon people in Europe were eating ice and fruit. Then cream was put in the mix. More and more people ate it. Ice cream in the 1700s was a lot like it is now.

Nancy Johnson made the first ice cream freezer. That was in 1846. The freezer had a crank. The crank had to be turned. It had to be turned by hand, over and over. Anyone could buy a freezer. You could make ice cream on your own!

Jacob Fussell owned a dairy. He ended up with extra cream. What did he do with it? He sold ice cream. It was a big hit! It made him lots of money. It made him more money than the dairy did. Fussell built an ice cream **factory** in 1851. It was the first one in America.

A Cold Treat

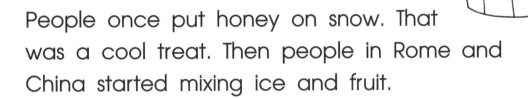

How old is ice cream? Who made it first? No one knows for sure.

People once put honey on snow. That was a cool treat. Then people in Rome and China started mixing ice and fruit.

Soon people in France were eating ice and fruit, too. In time, cream was added into the mix. Ice cream became more popular. By the 1700s, it was a lot like it is now.

Nancy Johnson made the first hand-cranked ice cream freezer in 1846. Anyone could buy a freezer. People began to make ice cream themselves.

Jacob Fussell owned a dairy. There was always cream left over. Fussell never knew what to do with it. He tried using it to make ice cream. It was a great hit. Fussell made lots of money selling ice cream. He made more than he did with his dairy! So he built America's first ice cream **factory**. That was in 1851.

A Cold Treat

How old is ice cream? Who made it first? No one knows for sure.

People once put honey on snow. That was a cool treat. Then people in Rome and China started mixing ice and fruit.

Soon people in France were eating ice and fruit, too. Eventually cream was added as an ingredient. Ice cream became popular. By the 1700s, ice cream was like it is today.

Nancy Johnson made the first hand-cranked ice cream freezer in 1846. Anyone could buy one of her freezers. People began to make ice cream themselves.

Jacob Fussell owned a dairy in Baltimore, Maryland. There was always extra cream left over. Fussell never knew what to do with it. He tried using it to make ice cream. It was a great hit. He made lots of money selling ice cream. He made more than he did with his dairy! In 1851, Fussell built the first ice cream **factory** in America.

Name _____ Date _____

Use what you read in the passage to answer the questions.

1. What is a **factory**?

_____

_____

2. Where does cream come from?

_____

_____

3. Who was Nancy Johnson? What is she famous for?

_____

_____

4. Who was Jacob Fussell? What is he famous for?

_____

_____

5. How did Jacob Fussell use his brain to make money?

_____

_____

6. Why did the author write about ice cream—to inform or to entertain?

_____

_____

How Much Money?

Today is the fair! A girl at the fair paints pictures. The girl paints face pictures. A picture costs fifty cents.

Jamal has coins. He has fifty cents in coins.

Allie has fifty pennies. Fifty pennies is equal to fifty cents.

Raul has ten nickels. Ten nickels is equal to fifty cents.

Ming has five dimes. Five dimes is equal to fifty cents.

John has two quarters. Two quarters is equal to fifty cents.

Luz has a handful of coins. She has enough to get a picture. What coins might she have?

Jamal gets a star on his face. He wants to get one more. Does he have enough money?

How Much Money?

Today is the fair! One person at the fair paints pictures. The person paints pictures on faces. A picture costs fifty cents.

Jamal has coins. He has fifty cents.

Allie has fifty pennies. One penny is equal to one cent.

Raul has ten nickels. One nickel is equal to five cents. Ten nickels is equal to fifty cents.

Ming has five dimes. One dime is equal to ten cents.

John has two quarters. One quarter is equal to twenty-five cents. Two quarters is equal to fifty cents.

Luz has different coins. Luz can get a picture. What coins might she have?

The person paints a star for Jamal. Now Jamal wants to get another picture. Does he have enough money?

How Much Money?

Today is the county fair! An artist at the fair is painting pictures on people's faces for fifty cents each.

Jamal has fifty cents in coins.

Allie has fifty pennies. One penny is equal to one cent. Fifty pennies is equal to fifty cents.

Raul has ten nickels. One nickel is equal to five cents. Ten nickels is equal to fifty cents.

Ming has five dimes. One dime is equal to ten cents. Five dimes is equal to fifty cents.

John has two quarters. One quarter is equal to twenty-five cents. Two quarters is equal to fifty cents.

Luz has a handful of different coins. She has enough to get a picture. What combination of coins might Luz have?

The artist painted a star on Jamal's face, but now Jamal wants to get another picture. Does he have enough money?

●●●   *Meaningful Mini-Lessons & Practice: Comprehension Grade 2 • © Newmark Learning, LLC*

Name _____ Date _____

Use what you read in the passage to answer the questions.

1. How much is each painting?

_____

_____

2. Who has the most coins?

_____

_____

3. Why can't Jamal get another painting?

_____

_____

4. Why is it important to know how much each person has?

_____

_____

5. Why is it important to know how much each coin is worth?

_____

_____

6. What purpose did the author have in mind when writing this text?

_____

_____

Who Was Jackie Robinson?

Jackie Robinson was born in 1919. He was an African American baseball player. Life was hard for African Americans back then. They could not eat in some places. They had to sit at the back of buses. They could not play baseball on white teams.

That changed in 1947. Jackie Robinson joined the Dodgers. All the other players were white. It was hard for Jackie at first. Some of the players on his team were not nice to him. They did not want him to play with them. Some players tried to hurt him. People at the games shouted mean things. But Jackie did not say a word. He just played ball. He was a great player. He helped his team to win. The Dodgers went to the World Series that year. They won the Series in 1955.

Jackie Robinson died in 1972. African Americans had more **rights** by then. They did not have to sit at the back of a bus. They could eat anyplace. Thanks to Jackie, everyone got to play baseball!

Who Was Jackie Robinson?

Jackie Robinson was born in 1919. He was an African American baseball player. In those days, life was hard for African Americans. They could not eat in some places. They had to sit at the back of buses. They could not play baseball on white teams.

But that changed in 1947. Jackie Robinson joined the Dodgers. All the other players were white. It was hard for Jackie at first. Some of the players on his team were not nice to him and did not want to play on the same team. Some players tried to hurt him. People in the stands shouted mean things. But Jackie did not say a word. He just played ball, and he was great. He helped his team to win. The Dodgers went to the World Series that year. They won the Series in 1955.

Jackie Robinson died in 1972. By then, African Americans had more **rights**. They did not have to sit at the back of a bus. They could eat anyplace. And, thanks to Jackie, everyone got to play baseball!

Who Was Jackie Robinson?

Jackie Robinson was born in 1919. Robinson was an African American baseball player. Life was hard for African Americans back then. They could not eat in some places, and they had to sit at the back of buses. They could play ball, but they could not play on white teams.

All that changed in 1947. Jackie Robinson joined the Dodgers, an all-white team. It was hard for Robinson at first. Some of the players on his team were not nice to him. They did not want him to play with them. Some players went as far as trying to hurt him. People in the stadium shouted mean things. But Robinson never said a word. He just played ball, and what a great player he was! He helped the Dodgers get to the World Series that year. They actually won the World Series in 1955.

Jackie Robinson died in 1972. By then, African Americans had the same **rights** as everyone else. And thanks to Jackie Robinson, everyone got to play baseball!

Name _____ Date _____

Use what you read in the passage to answer the questions.

1. Who was Jackie Robinson?

_____

_____

2. What was Robinson famous for?

_____

_____

3. Which baseball team did Robinson play on?

_____

_____

4. What are **rights**?

_____

_____

5. How did Robinson change history?

_____

_____

6. How did reading this biography help you better understand our society?

_____

_____

Are You Patriotic?

The world has many countries. Every country has **patriotic** citizens. Patriotic citizens are proud of their country. They also help their country. Patriotic citizens celebrate special holidays. People get together. They eat good food. They have parties. They go to parades, too.

Many countries have a flag. Patriotic citizens are proud of their flag. Many countries have a song, too. Patriotic citizens learn the words. Then they can sing the song.

Patriotic citizens do many things to help their country. They help make rules. Good citizens help pick leaders for their country. Patriotic citizens follow the rules. They try to change things to make life better.

You can be a patriotic citizen. Celebrate the holidays from your country. What does your flag look like? You can learn about the flag. You can learn what the colors mean. You can learn what the symbols mean. What is your country's song? You can learn the words. You can sing it, too.

●○○

Are You Patriotic?

The world has many countries. Every country has **patriotic** citizens. Patriotic citizens are proud of their country. They also help their country. Patriotic citizens celebrate special holidays. People get together and eat good food. Sometimes they have parties and parades, too.

Many countries have a flag. Patriotic citizens are proud of their flag. Many countries have a song, too. Patriotic citizens can sing the words to their country's song.

Patriotic citizens do many things to help their country. They help make rules for their country. Good citizens help pick leaders for their country. Patriotic citizens follow the rules and try to change things to make life better.

You can be a patriotic citizen. Celebrate the holidays from your country. What does your flag look like? You can learn about the flag. You can learn what the colors and symbols mean. What is your country's song? You can learn the words and sing it, too.

Are You Patriotic?

The world has many countries. Every country has **patriotic** citizens. Patriotic citizens are proud of their country and help their country as well. Patriotic citizens celebrate special holidays. People get together and eat good food and have parties. They go to parades, too.

Many countries have a flag. Patriotic citizens are proud of their flag. Many countries have a song, too. Patriotic citizens know the words to their country's song and can sing it.

Patriotic citizens do many things to help their country. They help make rules for their country. Good citizens help pick leaders for their country. Patriotic citizens follow the rules and try to change things to make life better.

You can be a patriotic citizen. Celebrate the holidays from your country. What does your flag look like? You can learn about the flag and what the colors and symbols mean. What is your country's song? You can learn the words to the song, and sing it, too.

Name _____ Date _____

Use what you read in the passage to answer the questions.

1. What does **patriotic** mean?

_____

_____

2. What are three ways you can show you
are patriotic?

_____

_____

3. Why is it a good idea to know what the colors
and symbols on your flag mean?

_____

_____

4. What is one way you celebrate a holiday from
your country?

_____

_____

5. How do good citizens help their government?

_____

_____

6. How might you learn the words to your
country's song?

_____

_____

Unit 7 Mini-Lesson
Science

What is science?

Science helps us understand the world around us. To be a part of society, we must know some science. As examples, in order to cook dinner, you have to understand hot and cold. To choose to eat an apple rather than a bag of chips, you may have to know and think about nutrition.

What is the purpose of a science text?

A science text gives us information about the physical world around us. Life Science studies the living things on Earth. Earth Science is the study of the earth as well as things in outer space. Physical Science involves the study of nonliving things in our world.

Who is the audience for a science text?

Anyone who is interested in the physical world around us. As students in school, we read science texts to learn about the creatures and vegetation that inhabit Earth, and possibly space.

How do you read a science text?

You don't have to read it from beginning to end.
1. Look at the Table of Contents or the Index to see what's included.
2. Scan possible chapters or sections of the text, and look at the headings and subheadings.
3. Look for charts, drawings, photographs, and other graphics.
4. Look for a glossary at the back of the text that explains the terms.

Meaningful Mini-Lessons & Practice: Comprehension Grade 2 • © Newmark Learning, LLC

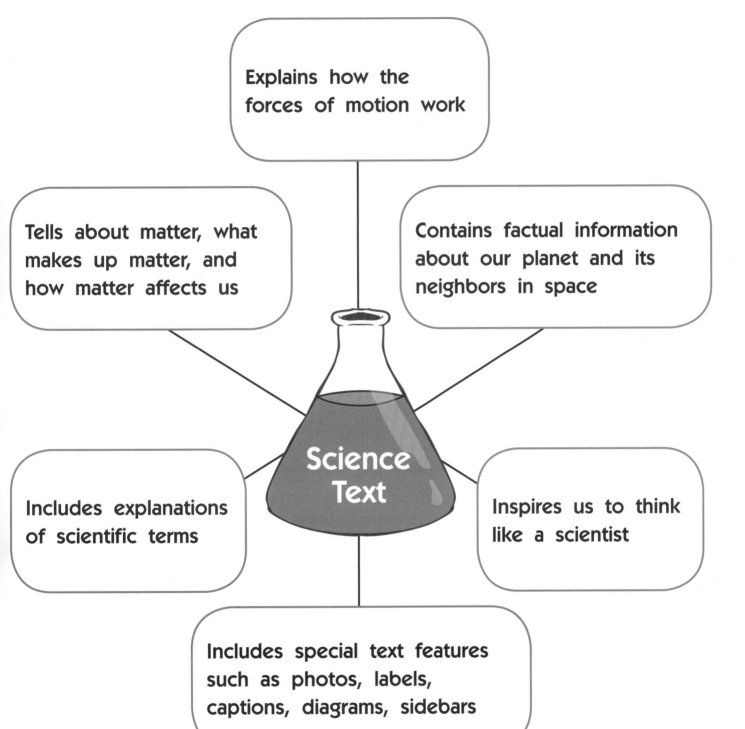

Explains how the forces of motion work

Tells about matter, what makes up matter, and how matter affects us

Contains factual information about our planet and its neighbors in space

Includes explanations of scientific terms

Science Text

Inspires us to think like a scientist

Includes special text features such as photos, labels, captions, diagrams, sidebars

Properties of Matter

Everything is made of matter. Matter takes up space. Matter has **properties**. These properties can change.

Size is one property. Size tells how big or small something is. You can change the size of matter. You can slice matter to make it smaller. You can shred matter to make it smaller, too.

Shape is another property. You can change the shape of matter. You can roll it to make it flat or form it into a ball.

Temperature is a property, too. Temperature is how hot or cold matter is. You can change the temperature of matter. You can make matter hotter. You can make matter colder. If some matter gets hot enough, the matter could melt. It could become a liquid. If some matter gets cold enough, the matter could freeze. It becomes a solid.

Where would we be without matter?

solid   **liquid**   **gas**

●○○

Properties of Matter

Everything is made of matter. Matter takes up space. Matter has certain **properties**. The properties of matter can change.

Size is a property of matter. Size tells how big or small something is. You can change the size of matter. You can slice or shred matter to make it smaller.

Shape is another property of matter. You can change the shape of matter. You can roll it to make it flat or form it into a ball.

Temperature is another property of matter. Temperature is how hot or cold matter is. You can change the temperature of matter. You can make it hotter. You can make it colder. If some matter gets hot enough, it could melt. It could become a liquid. If some matter gets cold enough, it could freeze. It could become a solid.

You can change the properties of matter. You can change its size, its shape, and its temperature.

solid   **liquid**   **gas**

Where would we be without matter?

Properties of Matter

Everything in the universe is made of matter. Matter takes up space. Matter has certain **properties**. The properties of matter can change.

Size is one of the properties of matter. Size tells how big or small something is. You can change the size of matter. You can slice or shred matter to make it smaller.

Shape is another property of matter. You can change the shape of matter. For instance, you can roll matter to make it flat or crumple it into a ball.

Temperature is yet another property of matter. Temperature is how hot or cold matter is. You can change the temperature of matter by making it hotter or colder. If some matter gets hot enough, it could melt, or become a liquid. If some matter gets cold enough, it could freeze, or become a solid.

Where would we be without matter?

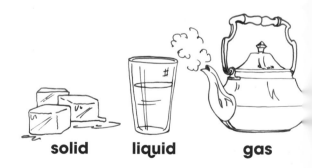

solid   **liquid**   **gas**

⬤⬤⬤

Name _____ Date _____

Use what you read in the passage to answer the questions.

1. What are **properties**?

_____

_____

2. What are three properties of matter?

_____

_____

3. What happens when matter is heated?

_____

_____

4. What happens when matter is made colder?

_____

_____

5. Are the statements in the text factual or are they opinions? What makes you say so?

_____

_____

6. Is matter important? What makes you think so?

_____

_____

Movement

Everything moves. It might be a small movement. It might be a big movement. Are you still moving if you stand still? The answer is yes. You are standing on the earth. The earth is always turning. Turning is movement.

The blood in your veins is moving. Your heart is always pumping. Pumping shows movement. So you are always moving! You are always in motion!

You can move your body. You can move things, too. What makes motion happen? **Force** is what makes motion happen. Let's look at some examples.

You use force to push. Jason pushes the scooter. The scooter moves.

You use force to pull. Steve pulls a wagon. The wagon moves.

How else can you use force to make motion?

●○○

Movement

Everything moves. It might be a small movement or it might be a big movement. If you are standing still, are you still moving? The answer is yes. You are standing on the earth. The  earth is always turning. Turning is movement.

The blood in your veins is moving. Your heart is always pumping, and pumping shows movement. So you are always moving! You are always in motion!

You can move your body, and you can move things, too. What makes motion happen? **Force** is what makes motion happen. Let's look at some examples.

You use force to push. For example, Jason pushes the scooter and the scooter moves.

You use force to pull. For example, Steve pulls a wagon and the wagon moves.

How else can you use force to make motion?

Movement

Did you know you are still moving even if you stand still? You are standing on the earth, and the earth is always turning. You turn with the earth. Turning is movement.

The blood in your veins is moving, and your heart is always pumping. Pumping shows movement, so your insides are always moving! You are always in motion!

You can move your body, and you can move things, too. You use **force** to make motion happen. Let's look at some examples.

Pushing takes force. Jason pushes the scooter and the scooter moves.

Pulling takes force. Steve pulls a wagon and the wagon moves.

How else can you use force to make motion?

Name _____ Date _____

Use what you read in the passage to answer the questions.

1. What is **force**?

_____

_____

2. What is the main idea of this passage?

_____

_____

3. Who in the passage used force? How do you know?

_____

_____

4. Is this passage facts and information or funny and entertaining?

_____

_____

5. How does the author explain how you can be standing still and yet moving?

_____

_____

6. Give an example of how you can use force to make motion.

_____

_____

Our Solar System

What is the solar system?
The sun is in our solar system.
So are the planets. Earth is one of
those planets. Let's find out more.

The Sun

The sun is a star. It is a lot like any star in
the sky. It is a ball of burning **gas**. But our
sun is special in one way. It is much closer
to us than any other star. Many stars are
much bigger than the sun. Our sun looks big
because it is so close.

The Planets

Our solar system has eight planets. All of them
move around the sun. Some planets are made
mostly of rock. Other planets are made of
gas. Some planets are very hot. Other planets
are very cold. Earth has a moon. Some
planets do not have moons.

Is there life on the other planets? We do not
know. Someday we hope to find out!

Our Solar System

What is the solar system?
The sun is in our solar system.
So are the planets that move around it.
Earth is one of those planets.

The Sun

The sun is a star much like any star in the sky. It is a ball of burning **gas**. But our sun is special in one way. It is much closer to us than any other star. Many stars are much bigger than the sun. But the sun looks huge because it is so close.

The Planets

There are eight planets in our solar system. All of them move around the sun. The planets are different in many ways. Some are made mostly of rock. Others are made of gas. Some are very hot. Others are very cold.

The planets are different in another way, too. Some have moons, but some do not.

We are not sure if there is life on the other planets. Someday we hope to find out!

Our Solar System

What is the solar system?
The solar system is made up
of the sun and all of the planets and
moons that move around it. Earth is one of
those planets.

The Sun

The sun is a star much like any star in the
sky. It is a ball of burning **gas**. But our sun is
special because It is much closer to us than
any other star. Many stars are much bigger
than the sun. But the sun looks huge to us
because it is so close.

The Planets

There are eight planets in our solar system.
All of them move around the sun. But the
planets are different in many ways. Some are
made mostly of rock, and others are made of
gas. Some are very hot, but others are very
cold. Some have moons, but some do not.

We are not sure if there is life on the other
planets. Someday we hope to find out!

Name _____ Date _____

Use what you read in the passage to answer the questions.

1. Why are some words in boldface type?

_____

_____

2. What is a "ball of burning **gas**"?

_____

_____

3. Why does the sun seem so big to us?

_____

_____

4. What are two ways that the planets are the same? Two ways they are different?

_____

_____

5. Is the kind of gas in the passage different than the gas you put in a car?

_____

_____

6. How do you think the author feels about finding out if there is life on other planets? Why do you think that?

_____

_____

What Do Scientists Do?

What do scientists do? Scientists study things. They **investigate**. They follow steps.

Scientists use their senses to observe the world. You can use your sense of smell to observe fruit. Fruit has a scent, or odor.

Scientists ask questions after they observe. What can you ask about your sense of smell?

They choose a question to look into. They think about what they know. Then they make a smart guess about the answer.

Next, they plan how to test their guess, or prediction. They gather what they need. Then they test their guess. You can test yours, too.

Scientists follow steps. You followed steps, too. You learned about your sense of smell. You are a scientist!

What Do Scientists Do?

What do scientists do? Scientists study things. They **investigate** by following specific steps in order.

Scientists use their senses to observe. You can use your sense of smell to observe fruit. Fruit has a scent, or odor.

After scientists observe, they ask questions. What questions can you ask to learn more about your sense of smell?

Scientists choose a question to study. They use what they already know to predict the answer.

Next, scientists plan how to test their prediction. They gather what they need and test their prediction. You can test your prediction, too.

Scientists follow steps when they study something. You followed steps, too. You learned about your sense of smell. You are a scientist!

What Do Scientists Do?

What do scientists do? Scientists **investigate** things by following specific steps in a certain order.

Scientists use their senses to observe. You can use your sense of smell to observe fruit. Fruits have a scent, or odor.

After scientists observe, they ask questions. What questions can you ask to learn more about your sense of smell?

Scientists choose a question to investigate and use what they already know to predict the answer.

Next, scientists plan how to test their prediction. They gather what they need and test their prediction. You can test your prediction, too.

Scientists follow steps when they investigate. You followed steps, too. You learned about your sense of smell. You are a scientist!

●●●

Name _____ Date _____

Use what you read in the passage to answer the questions.

1. What does **investigate** mean?

_____

_____

2. Name some steps scientists use to investigate.

_____

_____

3. Why would you investigate something?

_____

_____

4. Do you think scientists always follow the same order of steps? What might happen if they didn't?

_____

_____

5. Name a sense you could use to investigate a fruit.

_____

_____

6. What does the author mean when he or she says "You are a scientist!"?

_____

_____

Overview III: Introduction to Opinion/Argument

What Is It?

What is an argument?

An argument is a form of writing that tries to convince the reader to do or believe something. The text argues the writer's opinion on a topic. A good argument includes smart reasons and facts.

Examples

- Advertisements
- Book reviews
- Commentaries
- Letters to the editor
- Personal essays
- Persuasive letters

What are some examples of argument text?

Purpose

What is the purpose of an argument?
The writer wants to:
- change the reader's point of view
- get the reader to act on something
- have the reader accept the writer's explanation

Audience

Who is the audience for an argument?
The audience is anyone that the writer thinks he or she has a chance of persuading! They can be students, business leaders, politicians, or neighbors and friends.

How to Use It

How do you read an argument?
1. Look for the issue.
2. What does the writer think about it?
3. Does the writer give good reasons?
4. Do you feel the same way?

What are common features of an opinion/argument?

Uses powerful words
to influence the reader

Suggests solutions
or actions

Has a specific
audience in mind

Opinion/
Argument

Has a strong position,
or point of view

Uses facts and evidence
to make a case

Persuasive Letters

What is a persuasive letter?

A persuasive letter is a letter that tries to convince readers to believe or do something. A persuasive letter has a strong point of view. It includes facts and examples to support an opinion. It usually suggests a solution.

What is the purpose of a persuasive letter?

People write persuasive letters to change the minds of their readers. They want readers to see their point of view. They may want readers to take action, too.

Who is the audience for a persuasive letter?

People write persuasive letters to make other people understand their views. For example, people might write to a leader about a law they don't agree with. The writer might want the leader to change the law.

How do you read a persuasive letter?

1. What is this writer's position, or opinion?
2. Does he or she support it with facts and good reasons?
3. Do I agree with him?

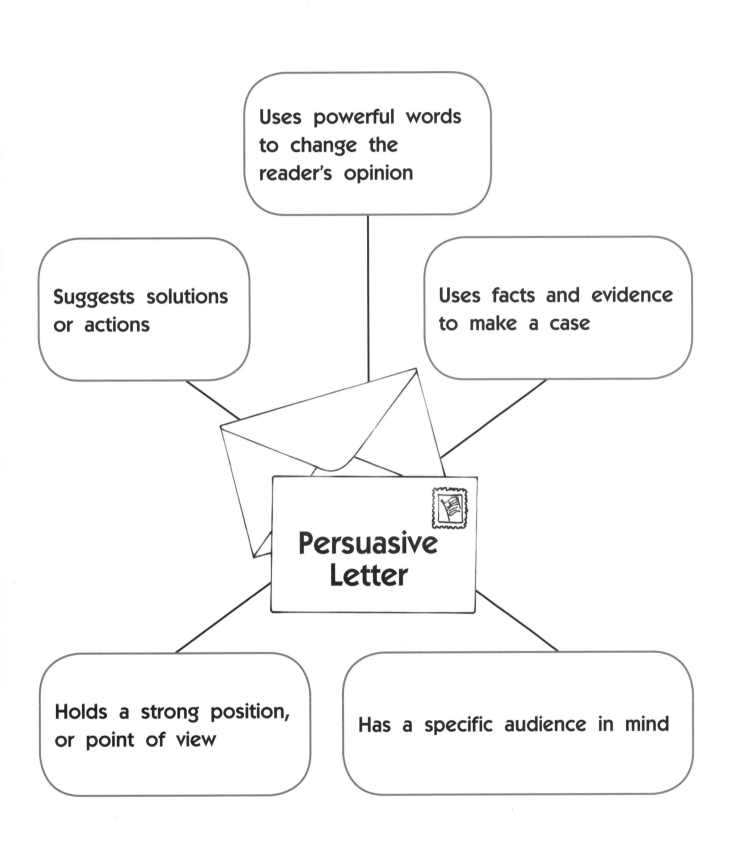

Uses powerful words to change the reader's opinion

Suggests solutions or actions

Uses facts and evidence to make a case

Persuasive Letter

Holds a strong position, or point of view

Has a specific audience in mind

No More Junk Food Ads

Dear Senator,

We should all care about what children eat. Wrong foods can be bad. Kids can get sick. They can gain weight. They can die young. People who make junk food have ads. The ads are on TV and radio. The ads are on the Internet, too. Kids see these.

Many ads are made for children. Cartoons are used in the ads. Children love these characters. So they think the food must be good. I think ads like this are wrong!

We need a new law. It should stop junk food ads. We should get more healthy food ads. The health of our children is in your hands. Please make a law against these ads.

Sincerely,

Juan Santiago

●○○

No More Junk Food Ads

Dear Senator,

We should all care about the kinds of foods children eat. Eating the wrong foods can be very bad. Children can get sick. They can gain too much weight. They can die young. But the junk food companies have nonstop ads on TV and radio. They have them on the Internet, too. Many seem made for children.

Cartoon characters are used in the ads. Children love these characters. So they think the food must be good. We need a new law. This law should stop junk food ads for children. Show more healthy foods!

The health of our children is in your hands. Please help make a law against these ads.

Sincerely,

Juan Santiago

No More Junk Food Ads

Dear Senator,

We should all be concerned about the foods children eat. Eating the wrong foods can be very dangerous. People can get sick. They can gain too much weight. They can die young. But the people who make junk foods promote them on TV, radio, and the Internet.

Some companies use cartoon characters in their ads. Children love these characters, so they think the food must be good. I think this is wrong. We need a new law that limits junk food ads for children. Maybe then companies might make more healthy foods for kids.

The health of our children is in your hands. Please make junk food ads illegal.

Sincerely,

Juan Santiago

●●●

Name _____ Date _____

Use what you read in the passage to answer the questions.

1. What is the writer's opinion about junk food ads?

_____

_____

2. What does the writer want the senator to do?

_____

_____

3. What reason does the writer give about wanting to limit junk food ads?

_____

_____

4. What bad effects does the writer say that junk food causes?

_____

_____

5. Why do you think the companies use children's cartoon characters?

_____

_____

6. What does "in your hands" mean?

_____

_____

Let's Recycle!

Dear Principal,

Earth Day is a week away. We are reading about Earth. We want to show that we care. We want to help at school. We have a great idea.

We want to save paper. We want to save more trees. We want to recycle! My class can **sponsor** a bake sale. We can use the money we make to buy bins. We need one small bin for each class.

We will also pick up the paper trash. We will take it to the janitor each day. He can put it out for pickup.

It will cost $350 to buy the bins.

We want to stop wasting paper. It is the right thing to do!

Sincerely,

Amy Adams

●○○   *Meaningful Mini-Lessons & Practice: Comprehension Grade 2* • © Newmark Learning, LLC

Let's Recycle!

Dear Principal,

Earth Day is a week away. We are reading about Earth. We want to show that we care. We want to help at school. We have a great idea.

We want to save paper. We want to save more trees. We want to recycle! My class can **sponsor** a bake sale next week. We can use the money we make to buy bins. We need one small bin for each class.

We will also pick up the paper trash. Two students in my class will take it to the janitor each day. He can put it out for pickup.

It will cost $350 to buy the bins.

We really want to stop wasting paper. We think this is the right thing to do!

Sincerely,

Amy Adams

Let's Recycle!

Dear Principal,

Earth Day is just a week away. My class has been reading about our planet. We want to show our concern about the environment. We want to take action, and we've got a great idea.

We want our school to stop wasting paper. We want to save more trees. We would like to buy recycling bins for our school. My class wants to **sponsor** a bake sale next week. We can use the money we make. We will need one small bin for each classroom.

We have looked at prices for recycling bins. We think we will need about $350 to buy the bins for our school. We will also volunteer to pick up the paper garbage. Every day, two students in my class will take it to the janitor. Recycling at our school is the right thing to do!

Sincerely,

Amy Adams

●●●

Name _____ Date _____

Use what you read in the passage to answer the questions.

1. What does the writer think the problem is?

_____

_____

2. What does the writer want to do about the problem?

_____

_____

3. What does **sponsor** mean?

_____

_____

4. What does the writer want the principal to do?

_____

_____

5. Name a fact, or piece of evidence, that the writer gives.

_____

_____

6. Do you think the principal will agree? Why or why not?

_____

_____

Book Reviews

What is a book review?

A book review judges a book. The reviewer describes what happens in the book. The reviewer shares his or her opinions about the book. The reviewer uses details from the book to support his or her opinions.

What is the purpose of a book review?

Many people want to know about a book before they read it. They want to know what the book is about and if it is the "right" book for them. A book review helps readers decide whether or not to read a book.

Who is the audience for a book review?

The reviewer writes to all of the people who might want to read the book that he or she is reviewing.

How do you read a book review?

Ask yourself:

1. *What is the plot? Who are the characters? What is the topic of the book?*
2. *Did it interest the reviewer? How can I tell?*
3. Think about how the reviewer rated the book. *What did the reviewer like? What did he or she not like?*
4. *Did he or she give good reasons for his or her opinions?*
5. *Do I want to read the book now?*

Analyzes characters, plot, and ideas

Includes a summary of the book

Evaluates the characters, plot, and ideas

Book Review

Gives the title and information about the author

Identifies the book's strengths and weaknesses

Identifies the intended audience

The Three Little Pigs

Three pigs are brothers. Each pig builds a house. A wolf comes around. Only one pig can outsmart him.

The story has no drama or suspense. The pigs are not very interesting. And the big bad wolf is not so bad.

No one knows who wrote the story. It was in a book of English fairy tales in the 1840s. Children have been reading it ever since.

Millions of people know the story. Children can tell it word for word. That is part of the problem. The story is boring. But very young readers may like it. Older readers will roll their eyes. They want action! The wolf cannot blow the third pig's house down. The pig knows it. So the pig tries to trick him.

The end is happy. The story has a lesson for the reader. Make sure your home is strong!

The Three Little Pigs

Three pigs are brothers. Each builds a house. A "big bad wolf" comes around. Only one can outsmart him.

Do not read this story if you are looking for drama and suspense. The pigs are not very interesting. And the big bad wolf isn't so bad.

No one knows who wrote the story. It was in a book of English fairy tales in the 1840s. It has been popular ever since.

Millions of people know the story. Children can tell it word for word. That may be part of the problem. The story is boring and repetitive. Very young readers may enjoy it. Older readers will roll their eyes. They want action! The third pig knows that the wolf can't blow down his brick house. So the pig tries to trick him.

Readers will cheer at the ending. The story offers a good tip. Make sure you have a strong home!

The Three Little Pigs

Three pigs are brothers. Each builds a house. A "big bad wolf" comes around, but only one pig is intelligent enough to outsmart the wolf.

Warning: Do not read this story if you are looking for drama and suspense. Those pigs are boring, and the big bad wolf isn't so bad.

No one knows who wrote "The Three Little Pigs." The story was in a book of English fairy tales in the 1840s. It is still popular today.

Millions of people know "The Three Little Pigs." Young children can tell the story word for word. That may be part of the problem. The story is boring and repetitive. Readers in the under-five age group may enjoy it. Older readers will roll their eyes. They want action! The third pig knows that the wolf can't blow down his brick house. The pig tries to trick him.

I won't spoil the ending, but readers will cheer. The story delivers an important message: Make sure you have a strong home!

Name _____ Date _____

Use what you read in the passage to answer the questions.

1. Does the critic say what the story is about?

_____

_____

2. What are two words the critic uses to describe the story?

_____

_____

3. What does the critic like about the story? What words tell you this?

_____

_____

4. What does the critic not like about the story? What words tell you this?

_____

_____

5. Did the critic make you want to read the story or not read it? Why?

_____

_____

6. Do you agree with the critic's review? Why or why not?

_____

Cinderella

"Cinderella" is a great fairy tale. It has everything that a story should have. The girl is kind. She lives with an evil stepmother. There are two evil stepsisters. The girl has a fairy godmother. She meets a handsome prince. There is love. There is magic. And there is a happy ending.

The story goes back many years. Egypt had a story like it. China did, too. The story was told around the world. Many cultures have a "Cinderella" story. It has been made into movies, too. It was even made into a **musical**. That is a show full of songs.

Charles Perrault wrote the story in 1697. It is still worth reading. Children and adults all like the story. The story gives people hope. It reminds us that good things can happen to people who work hard. And that good things can happen even if the world seems unfair. It reminds us that there IS such a thing as a happy ending!

Cinderella

"Cinderella" is a great fairy tale. It has everything a story should have. The girl is kind. She lives with an evil stepmother and two evil stepsisters. She has a fairy godmother. She meets a handsome prince. There is love and there is magic. And there is a happy ending.

The story goes back thousands of years. Ancient Egypt had a story like it. So did China. The story spread around the world. Many cultures have a "Cinderella" tale. It has been made into movies, too. It has even been a Broadway **musical**. That is a show full of songs.

Charles Perrault wrote the story in 1697. It is worth reading. Children and adults all like reading the story. Cinderella's story gives people hope. It tells us that good things can happen to people who work hard. They can happen no matter how unfair things are. The story reminds us that there IS such a thing as a happy ending!

Cinderella

One of the best fairy tales ever is "Cinderella." It has everything a story should have. There is a kindhearted girl. She lives with an evil stepmother and two evil stepsisters. She has a fairy godmother, which means magic is involved. And she meets a handsome prince. Best of all, there's a happy ending.

The story goes back thousands of years. Ancient Egypt had a story like it. So did China. The story was so good that it spread from one country to another. Many cultures have a tale like "Cinderella." The story has been made into movies, too. It has even been a Broadway **musical**—a show full of singing and dancing.

Charles Perrault wrote the story in 1697. It is worth reading. Children and adults all enjoy reading this story. Cinderella's story gives everyone hope. When things are bad, something good can happen, especially to a good person who works hard, no matter what happens or how unfair things are. The story reminds us that happy endings are possible!

Meaningful Mini-Lessons & Practice: Comprehension Grade 2 • © Newmark Learning, LLC

Name _____ Date _____

Use what you read in the passage to answer the questions.

1. What kind of story is "Cinderella"?

_____

_____

2. What is a **musical**?

_____

_____

3. What does the critic say the story is about?

_____

_____

4. What does the critic like about the story? What words tell you this?

_____

_____

5. Is there anything that the critic does not like about the story? If so, what? How can you tell?

_____

_____

6. What phrases does the critic use to tell us his or her opinion about the story?

_____

_____

Advertisements

What is an advertisement?

An advertisement, or "ad," is a form of persuasive text. It may include writing, photos, or drawings, or all three.

What is the purpose of an advertisement?

People write advertisements to sell something. The purpose of an ad is to talk you into buying, doing, or using a product or service. Ads often try to entertain people, or make them laugh. The ad writer wants you to remember to buy the product when you go to the store, or call them when you need a service like theirs.

Who is the audience for an advertisement?

The audience for an advertisement is a person who has money to buy things. The audience depends on what's being sold. It also depends on where the ad is printed. If the ad is in a kids' magazine, the ad will try to appeal to a young audience.

How do you read an advertisement?

Pay attention to the product or service being sold and how the writer is trying to sell it. Does the ad writer do a good job? Does the writer convince you that you want or perhaps even *need* the product?

Meaningful Mini-Lessons & Practice: Comprehension Grade 2 • © Newmark Learning, LLC

Describes a product or service

Tells name of product and where to buy it

Written with the buyer or user in mind

Advertisement

Tries to be catchy or funny so you will remember the product or service

May include awards or prizes that the product has won

Tells why a product or service is better than the others

Winter Warming Suit

Do you live in a cold **climate**? Do you hate coats and scarves? What about boots, mittens, and hats? Is it hard to move once you are dressed? We have the answer!

Get our Winter Warming Suit! We have tested it in the coldest parts of the world. But you can get it here now!

Plug in the suit. It takes 15 minutes to heat. Slip it on over your clothes. You'll stay warm for hours! The suit fits in its own small pouch. It is small enough to fit in your backpack!

It is light! It is easy to put on! You will never want to be without it! And it costs only three payments of $9.99 each.

So call us right now. Or contact us online. But hurry! Our Winter Warming Suits are flying off the shelves!

Get yours today!

Winter Warming Suit

Do you live in a cold **climate**?
Do you hate wearing coats
and scarves? What about
boots, mittens, and hats? Is it hard to
move around once you're dressed?

We have the answer!

Get our Winter Warming Suit! It's been tested
in the coldest places in the world. But you
can get it here for the very first time!

Just plug the suit into an outlet. It takes
15 minutes to work. Slip the suit on over your
clothes. You'll stay warm for hours! The suit fits
in its own zippered pouch. It's small enough to
fit in your backpack!

It's light! It's easy to put on! You'll never want
to be without it! And it costs only three easy
payments of $9.99 each.

So call us right now to place your order.
Or contact us online. But hurry! Our Winter
Warming Suits are flying off the shelves!

Get yours today!

Winter Warming Suit

Do you live in a cold **climate**?
Do you hate putting on jackets,
scarves, boots, mittens, and hats
to go play outside? Do you feel like it's
too hard to move around once you're dressed
to play outside? We have the answer!

Our Winter Warming Suit has been tested
in the coldest regions of the world. It's now
available in the U.S. for the very first time!

Just plug the Winter Warming Suit into any
electrical outlet. After 15 minutes, slip it over
your clothes. You'll stay warm for hours.
When you come inside, your Winter Warming
Suit fits in its convenient little zipper pouch.
It's small enough to fit in your backpack!

You'll never want to go a winter without this
product! And it's available to you for three
easy payments of $9.99 each.

So call us now to place your order. You can
also contact us online. But hurry! Our Winter
Warming Suits are flying off the shelves!

Get yours today!

●●●

Meaningful Mini-Lessons & Practice: Comprehension Grade 2 • © Newmark Learning, LLC

Name _____ Date _____

Use what you read in the passage to answer the questions.

1. What is being advertised?

_____

_____

2. What is the product supposed to do?

_____

_____

3. What does **climate** mean?

_____

_____

4. Does the ad make you want to buy the product? Why or why not?

_____

_____

5. What does the writer mean when he or she says "flying off the shelves"?

_____

_____

6. Do the opening lines in the text get your attention? Why or why not?

_____

_____

Brother Blocker 2.0

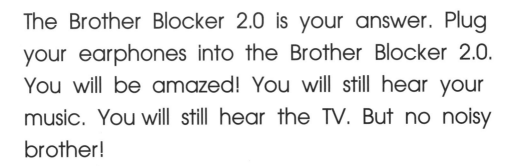

Do you have a brother? You know how annoying brothers can be. Age does not matter. Older or younger does not matter. They are whiny and bossy. They are gross. We know you have tried everything to ignore them.

The Brother Blocker 2.0 is your answer. Plug your earphones into the Brother Blocker 2.0. You will be amazed! You will still hear your music. You will still hear the TV. But no noisy brother!

The Brother Blocker 2.0 has had years of study. It has been tested in hundreds of families. And every one of those families had a brother in them. We know you will be happy! Or you get your money back!

So do not wait. Avoid the fights. Avoid the noise. Get your Brother Blocker 2.0 today!

Coming soon . . . The Sister Stopper 120. Watch for details!

●○○

Brother Blocker 2.0

Do you have a brother?

If you do, you know how annoying one can be. It doesn't matter how old they are. It doesn't matter if they're older than you or younger. They're whiny, bossy, and gross. We'll bet you've tried everything to ignore them. Everything, that is, until now.

The Brother Blocker 2.0 is your answer. Plug your earphones into the Brother Blocker 2.0. You'll be amazed! You'll still hear your music. You'll still hear the TV. But what you won't hear is your brother!

The Brother Blocker 2.0 has been tested in hundreds of families. We promise that you'll be happy! Or we'll give you your money back!

So don't wait. Avoid the fights. Avoid the noise. Get your Brother Blocker 2.0 today!

Coming soon . . . The Sister Stopper 120. Watch for details!

Brother Blocker 2.0

Have a brother, anyone?

If you have a brother,
you know how annoying one can be. Little
brothers, big brothers—it doesn't matter.
They're whiny, bossy, and gross. We'll bet
you've tried everything to ignore them or
drown them out.

The Brother Blocker 2.0 is the answer to your
problems. Plug your earphones Into the Brother
Blocker 2.0. You'll be amazed! You'll still be
able to hear your music. You'll still be able to
hear the TV. But what you won't hear is . . .
your brother!

The Brother Blocker 2.0 has been tested in
over 500 families, with brothers of all ages.
We promise you'll be amazed! In fact, we'll
give you your money back if you're not happy
with our product.

So don't wait. Avoid the fights. Avoid the
noise. Get your Brother Blocker 2.0 today!

And coming soon . . . The Sister Stopper 120.
Look for details in upcoming ads!

●●●   *Meaningful Mini-Lessons & Practice: Comprehension Grade 2* • © Newmark Learning, LLC

Name _____ Date _____

Use what you read in the passage to answer the questions.

1. What product is being advertised?

_____

_____

2. What is the product supposed to do?

_____

_____

3. Why should you buy the product?

_____

_____

4. Do the beginning and the end of the ad get your attention? Why or why not?

_____

_____

5. Does the ad make you want to buy the product? Why or why not?

_____

_____

6. Who is the intended audience for the ad? How do you know?

_____

_____

Answer Key

Unit 1 Personal Narratives I
page 13

1. Dad and me
2. It's a long uphill ride.
3. The tires are almost flat.
4. Breathing hard
5. A small stream
6. Sunny and warm

Unit 1 Personal Narratives II
page 17

1. To the dentist
2. Ellie
3. Afraid/worried/nervous
4. Bubble gum
5. Answers will vary.
6. Answers will vary.

Unit 2 Realistic Fiction I
page 23

1. Making a brick wall
2. A wall for his garden
3. A kind of mud used to make bricks
4. It helps to bake the bricks he is making.
5. Jamal wants to be Mr. Willis' helper.
6. The bricks might fall apart.

Unit 2 Realistic Fiction II
page 27

1. A house in a tree
2. Daytime/morning
3. Yes. He says he will help build it.
4. Saw boards
5. Answer could include saw, boards, nails, roof, hammer.
6. He wanted to sleep in his tree house.

Unit 3 Fairy Tales I
page 33

1. Jobs around the house
2. She sees the goldfish is starving, too.
3. The stepmother serves it for dinner.
4. Cinderella
5. Similar—Evil stepmother, mistreated stepdaughter, royal party, dress and slippers made by magic, stepdaughter marries royalty Not Similar—Bones of fish are magic instead of fairy godmother, no magic carriage, no deadline at midnight, no glass slippers, etc.
6. Answers may include goodness will be rewarded

 Meaningful Mini-Lessons & Practice: Comprehension Grade 2 • © Newmark Learning, LLC

Answer Key

Unit 3 Fairy Tales II
page 37

1. The lake dried up.
2. There were no fish for him to catch.
3. She felt sorry for the toad and felt a good deed would change their luck.
4. Her family saw a light in the night and thought it was a sign their daughter should marry the toad. (The toad had tied a lamp to a hawk's foot.)
5. Soo felt lucky to have a handsome and clever son, and the lake had filled with fish.
6. The story can't be true—toads don't talk, knock on doors, tie lamps to hawks, or turn into men!

Unit 4 Fables I
page 43

1. Sleeping
2. The lion thought it was funny that a tiny mouse said he might help him one day.
3. To chew on
4. The mouse gnawed through ropes to set the lion free.
5. They are both smart, both can talk, both have four legs and a tail, etc.
6. The moral is be kind to others and good things will happen to you later.

Unit 4 Fables II
page 47

1. To market
2. Sell the corn at the market
3. The angle of the hill makes it difficult to climb.
4. Similar—they are both hauling corn, both are being led to market, both are large animals. Different—the mule seems to be better at carrying heavy loads
5. The farmer takes all the baskets of corn off the horse and puts them on the mule, and leaves the horse to rest. He seems to be a kind person.
6. The moral seems to be if you don't help others when you have the chance, it will make things more difficult for you later.

Answer Key

Unit 5 Trickster Tales I
page 53

1. They could change themselves into anything they wished.
2. A character that likes to trick other characters. Also a kind of tale that features at least one trickster character.
3. He realizes that Raccoon has tricked Fox.
4. Answers will vary but should include no one getting hurt.
5. Answers may vary but Raccoon seems to be the best trickster because he tricked Fox.
6. The main characters are animals, it is short and funny, and it has a trickster who outwits another character.

Unit 5 Trickster Tales II
page 57

1. He hadn't eaten for 2 days and was hungry.
2. He wants him to pay for what he smells.
3. He drops coins on the table and then picks them back up.
4. Answers may vary but it seems mean to expect the poor man to wash dishes just to smell the soup.
5. Answers will vary but the author probably does not like greedy people because the greedy restaurant owner gets tricked.
6. There are no animals.

Unit 6 History
page 65

1. A factory is a building where things are made.
2. Cream comes from milk.
3. She invented the first ice cream maker.
4. He owned a dairy and built the first ice cream factory in America.
5. He figured out a way to use the extra cream he had—to make and sell ice cream.
6. The story is informative.

Unit 6 Economics
page 69

1. 50 cents
2. They all have 50 cents.
3. Because he only has enough money for one.
4. So they know what they can buy.
5. So you know how much money you have.
6. Answers will vary but may include teaching what coins have what value.

Answer Key

Unit 6 Biography
page 73

1. A baseball player
2. He was the first black player on a white team.
3. Dodgers
4. Rights are rules that say what freedoms we have.
5. He helped minorities to be allowed in sports.
6. Answers will vary but may include not realizing how blacks were treated in the past.

Unit 6 Government and Citizenship
page 77

1. Patriotic people are proud of their country and want to help it.
2. Answers could include: fly a flag at your home, go to parades, vote, know the history of your country, know the country's song, know the pledge of allegiance.
3. They can help you learn about your country.
4. Answers will vary.
5. Help pick leaders for the country by voting. Then follow the rules and try to make life better.
6. Answers may vary but might include reading it many times until you remember it.

Unit 7 Matter
page 83

1. Size, shape, and temperature
2. Size, shape, and temperature
3. It can melt and become a liquid.
4. It can freeze or become a solid.
5. Factual. Answers will vary.
6. Yes. Answers may vary but should include something about matter making up everything.

Unit 7 Forces and Motion
page 87

1. Force is used to make motion happen.
2. To show that things are always moving—even if you are standing still.
3. Jason pushing the scooter used the most force. Steve pulling the wagon used the least force.
4. Facts and information
5. Answers may vary but could include because the Earth is moving, or because your insides are always moving.
6. Answers will vary.

Answer Key

Unit 7 Earth and Space
page 91

1. Accept answers that indicate these are important words.
2. The sun
3. It is closer to us than any other star.
4. Same—They all move around the sun, and they are all very large objects. Different—Some are rock and some are gas, some hot and some cold, and some have moons and others don't.
5. Answers will vary.
6. According to the last sentence the author would like us to find out.

Unit 7 Scientific Investigations
page 95

1. To study things
2. Answers can include: observe, ask questions, choose a question to investigate, predict the answer, plan the test, gather what is needed, test.
3. To find the answer to a question.
4. Answers will vary but children should understand that the test won't go well if the steps are not followed.
5. Accept answers that include one or more senses.
6. By smelling something you performed a simple investigation—a bit like what scientists do.

Unit 8 Persuasive Letters I
page 103

1. Junk food ads should be against the law.
2. Pass a law to stop junk food ads for children
3. Eating the wrong foods can be dangerous.
4. People who eat a lot of junk food can gain weight, get sick, and possibly die young.
5. Children love the cartoon characters so they think the food must be good.
6. It is up to you to do something.

Unit 8 Persuasive Letters II
page 107

1. We are wasting paper.
2. Recycle paper at the school
3. Have, to make happen
4. The writer wants the principal to agree to her plan.
5. Answers will vary. Accept all statements of fact that are mentioned in the text.
6. Answers will vary. Accept well-supported answers.

Answer Key

Unit 9 Book Reviews I
pages 110–112

1. He says part of what it is about.
2. Answers could include boring and repetitive.
3. The critic likes the ending—says readers will cheer
4. He thinks it is only for the under-5 age group, because older readers will roll their eyes.
5. Answers will vary.
6. Answers will vary.

Unit 9 Book Reviews II
pages 114–116

1. Fairy tale
2. A show that includes songs
3. A kindhearted girl
4. Accept any of the following: the critic likes that it has a kindhearted girl, evil stepmother and stepsisters, a fairy godmother and a handsome prince.
5. The critic seems to like everything about the story.
6. Accept all reasonable answers.

Unit 10 Advertisements I
pages 120–122

1. A winter warming suit
2. Keep you warm for hours during winter
3. A place with a certain type of weather
4. Answers will vary. Accept all reasonable answers.
5. The suits will be selling quickly.
6. Answers will vary. Accept all reasonable answers.

Unit 10 Advertisements II
pages 124–126

1. The Brother Blocker 2.0
2. Block the noise of brothers
3. To solve the problem of annoying brothers
4. Answers will vary. Accept all reasonable answers.
5. Answers will vary. Accept all reasonable answers.
6. Anyone with a brother. Because of the first sentence.

Notes

Notes

_____

_____

_____

_____

_____

_____

_____

_____

_____

_____

_____

_____